How Artists View

# Families

**Karen Hosack**

Heinemann Library
Chicago, Illinois

Customer Service  888-454-2279
Visit our website at www.heinemannlibrary.com

Designed by Ron Kamen and Celia Floyd
Illustrations by Jo Brooker
Originated by Dot Gradations Ltd
Printed and bound in China by South China Printing Company

09 08 07 06 05
10 9 8 7 6 5 4 3 2 1

**Library of Congress Cataloging-in-Publication Data**
Hosack, Karen.
    Families / Karen Hosack.
        v. cm. -- (How artists view)
    Includes index.
    Contents: How artists see families -- Using line -- Using color -- Bold shapes -- A family likeness -- Painting people -- Giving people form -- Measuring heads and bodies -- Making babies look cute -- Expressing emotions -- Painting older people -- Royal Family portraits -- The wedding album.
    ISBN 1-4034-4851-5
    1. Family in art--Juvenile literature. 2. Art--Juvenile literature. [1. Family in art. 2. Art apprciation.] I. Title.
    N8217.F27H67 2004
    704.9'42--dc22
                                        2003026348

**Acknowledgments**

The author and publisher are grateful to the following for permission to reproduce copyright material:

Ancient Art and Architecture Collection Ltd pp. 6, 26 bottom; Art Institute of Chicago © Photo Scala, Florence p. 21 top; Art Institute of Chicago, IL / Bridgeman Art Library pp. 8, 9; Fitzwilliam Museum, Cambridge / Bridgeman Art Library p. 14 top; © DACS 2004 / Photo Walter Drayer, Zurich p. 7; Derby Museums and Art Gallery p. 22; Devonshire Collection, Chatsworth, reproduced by permission of the Duke of Devonshire and the Chatsworth Settlement Trustees p. 16; Harcourt Education Ltd/Tudor Photography p. 5 bottom, 25 x 3; Kunsthistorisches Museum, Vienna, Austria / Bridgeman Art Library p. 28; Mary Evans Picture Library p. 5 top; Metropolitan Museum of Art, New York / Bridgeman Art Library p. 29; © Museum of Fine Arts, Boston, Massachusetts, A. Shuman Collection / Bridgeman Art Library p. 12; Museum of London p. 14 bottom; National Gallery, London p. 20; National Portrait Gallery, London pp. 26 top, 27; Neidersachsische Landesmuseum, Hanover p. 24 (DACS); Nickelodeon Pictures / Ronald Grant p. 21 bottom; Private Collection / Christie's Images / Bridgeman Art Library p. 18 top; RMN – J G Berizzi – Le M: Louvre, Paris p. 23 x 2; © Romare Bearden Foundation / VAGA, New York / DACS, London 2004 / Collection of Halley K. Harrisburg and Michael Rosenfeld, New York p. 10; © Ron Mueck / Tate London 2004 p. 18 bottom; © Succession H Matisse / DACS 2004 / St Petersburg, Hermitage Museum © Photo Scala, Florence p. 4; © Succession Picasso / DACS 2004 / Bridgeman Art Library p. 11; © Tate London 2004 pp. 15, 17; © Thomas Struth / Tate London 2004 p. 13.

Cover photograph (*Three Fish* by Karolina Larusdottir, 1989) reproduced with permission of Noel Oddy Fine Art Galleries, London /Bridgeman Art Library.

Every effort has been made to contact copyright holders of any material reproduced in this book. Any omissions will be rectified in subsequent printings if notice is given to the publisher.

Some words are shown in bold, **like this.** You can find out what they mean by looking in the glossary.

# Contents

# How Artists See Families

*The Painter's Family* by Henri Matisse, 1911

For hundreds of years, artists have painted and taken photographs of families. Sometimes the artists were trying to show how important a family was. At other times, the paintings and photographs were made just so people would be able to remember their families growing up. Here, Matisse has painted his own family in their home. The children are playing a board game.

When the first camera was invented in 1827, it took more than eight hours to take a photograph. It would have been very expensive and only rich people could have recorded their families in this way. By the time the **Victorian** family above had their picture taken, cameras were a bit easier and cheaper to use.

### Digital pictures

This color photograph is very modern. It shows a family from our century. It was taken with a **digital camera.** The electronic image can be stored on a **CD-ROM** or even posted on a family website.

# Using Line

This picture was painted more than 2,000 years before cameras were invented. It shows people of different ages who look like each other. They were probably members of the same family from an ancient city called **Corinth.** The people are drawn with lines and then painted with blocks of **primary colors.** The figures are drawn from the side. The whole image looks very flat.

Corinthian plaque from Pitsa, Greece, around 540 B.C.E.

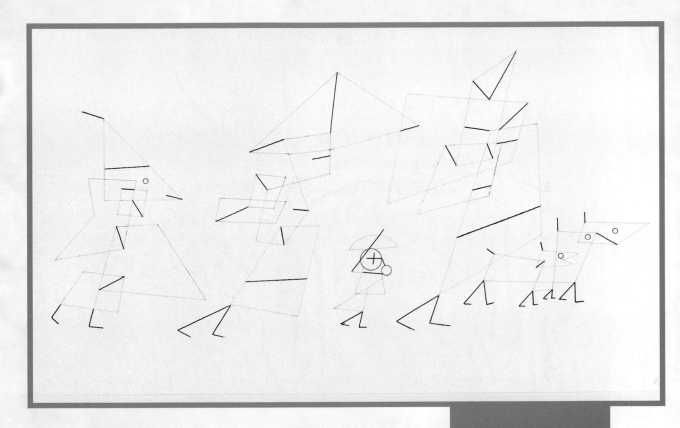

*Family Outing* by
Paul Klee, 1930

This family is also drawn from the side using
lines. This time the figures are not colored
in. The shapes are all lopsided triangles,
rectangles, and semi-circles. Paul Klee thought
hard about which shapes looked most like the
different parts of the body. Do you think he
got it right?

# Using Color

Here, Georges Seurat has painted families enjoying a Sunday afternoon together. Instead of mixing all his colors on his **palette,** the artist placed tiny dots of different colors next to each other on the **canvas.** When our eyes see these colors together, our brains mix them up so we see other colors. This gives the painting a sunny, hazy feel.

*A Sunday Afternoon on the Island of La Grande Jatte* by Georges Seurat, 1884–1886

*The Crystal Palace* by Camille Pissarro, 1871

Pissarro has painted families going to an exhibition in a big glass building in London. Look at how he only uses blocks of color to show their clothes and their hair. We can see many people walking away from us. Perhaps the artist wanted us to think we could follow them on their day out.

# Bold Shapes

The clothes the family are wearing in this picture are made up of different patterns. The basic shapes of the clothes are cut out and then arranged on the picture. This is called a **montage.** A montage can be made using scissors, paper, and glue. It can also be done on a computer.

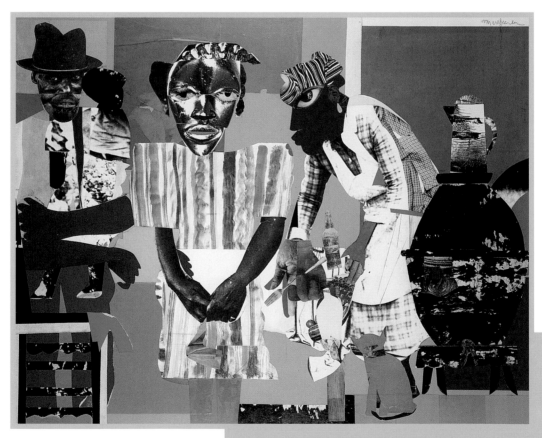

*Sunday Morning Breakfast* by Romare Howard Bearden, 1967

Pablo Picasso also used basic shapes in this picture of a mother and her son. First he drew the mother and son from different angles. Then he mixed the drawings together to make an **abstract** picture. The shapes are like jigsaw puzzle pieces. They fit together to show the mother and son holding each other closely.

# A Family Likeness

*Isaac Winslow and His Family*
by Joseph Blackburn, 1755

People belonging to the same family tend to look alike. Look at the people in this painting. The artist has painted their faces in detail to help show how similar they look.

This family had their group **portrait** taken by a photographer. They chose to have the picture taken at a beautiful spot in Japan, where they live. See how each member of the family looks similar. Do you look like people in your family?

The Shimada Family by Thomas Struth, 1986

# Painting People

It takes a long time to paint a **portrait** like this. In the 1700s, artists used dolls to replace the people for some of the time. This may be why these two people seem to be a bit stiff! Thomas Gainsborough only really needed to see Heneage Lloyd and his sister when he painted their faces.

*Heneage Lloyd and his Sister* by Thomas Gainsborough, mid-1750s

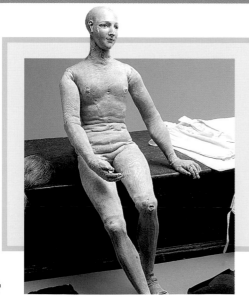

## Artists' dolls

Artists' dolls like this one were used by artists during the 1700s. The dolls showed the artist what people looked like when they were sitting or standing.

*Mr and Mrs Clark and Percy* by David Hockney, 1970

Mr. and Mrs. Clark probably **posed** at different times for their portraits. Percy the cat would have found it more difficult to stay still! *Mr and Mrs Clark and Percy* and *Heneage Lloyd and his Sister* were painted more than 200 years apart. From the portraits we can see how differently they lived, and how fashions have changed over the years.

# Giving People Form

**Did you know?**

Many artists use a layer of green paint underneath flesh colors to make people look more real. Joshua Reynolds never finished this painting. This means that we can see how the layers of paint were built up.

When Sir Joshua Reynolds painted this **portrait** he would have placed the people near a window. This would have made it easier for him to see the light and dark tones. Shadows and highlights give flat paintings the feeling of **depth.** This woman and her daughter are painted looking straight toward us. The light shining on their faces makes them look **three-dimensional.**

This sculpture of a **pregnant** woman is three-dimensional. You can walk all the way around it. It was made by **welding** pieces of metal together. The simple shapes of the pieces work together to make a very interesting **abstract** figure.

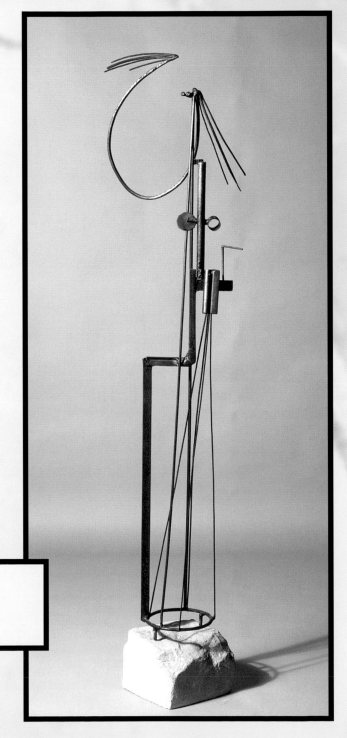

*Maternity* by Julio Gonzalez, 1934

# Measuring Heads and Bodies

When artists draw or make sculptures of people, they use the head as a unit of measurement. Count how many times the little dancer's head fits into the whole length of her body. It should be about seven times.

*Little Dancer Aged Fourteen* by Edgar Degas, around 1920–1921

*Ghost* by Ron Mueck, 1998

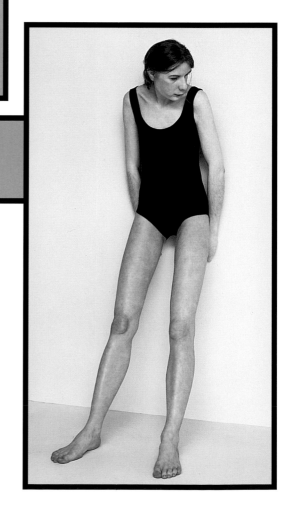

It is difficult to measure the height of the girl in Ron Mueck's sculpture because she is leaning against a wall. The sculpture is much bigger than a real-life girl, though her head is still the right size compared to her body. We say her head is in **proportion.**

# How artists measure heads and bodies

Try this technique for measuring people like artists do:

1. Place a pencil in your hand.

2. Hold your arm out straight.

3. Line the top of the pencil with the top of a person's head.

4. Mark the bottom of the head with your thumb.

5. Using the space between the tip of the pencil and your thumb, measure how many times it would fit into the full length of the person's body.

6. You can now use this measurement to draw a person in proportion. The number of times a person's head would fit into the length of his or her body is the number of times bigger you should draw his or her body compared to his or her head.

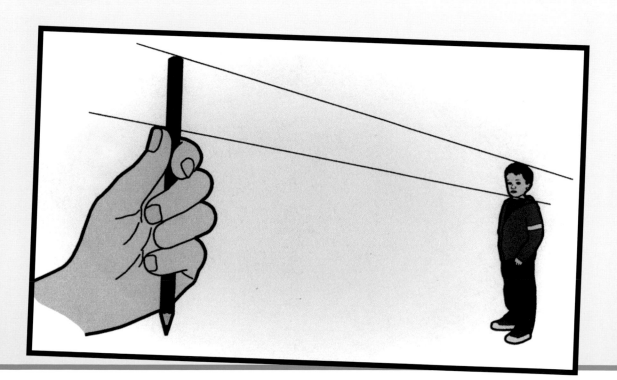

# Drawing Children

*The Graham Children* by William Hogarth, 1742

The children in this picture look grown up in their fancy clothes. In the 1700s, children were dressed to look like small adults. The baby is wearing a dress, but it is not a little girl. In those days, baby boys wore dresses too!

Mary Cassatt's painting shows a mother washing her child. Look at how large the child's head is compared to her body. Like all young animals, human children look cute. This makes people want to take care of them. Count how many times the child's head fits into the length of her body. It is much less than a teenager or an adult.

*The Bath* by Mary Cassatt, around 1891

## Cartoon babies

In cartoons, babies' heads are made even larger than in real life. This is why we find them so sweet. Their big eyes and chubby faces make them look even cuter than normal.

This is a **still** from the *Rugrats* cartoon.

# Expressing Emotions

Here we see people watching a man explaining how the **solar system** works. The children's expressions show they are fascinated. Joseph Wright used friends and their families to **pose** in many of his paintings. We do not know who the children in this picture are, but it is likely that they are brother and sister. This is because their faces are similar.

*The Orrery* by Joseph Wright of Derby, around 1764–1766

*Anger* by Charles Le Brun, around 1668

Charles Le Brun made these diagrams using just lines and tone to show what happens to people's faces when they make different expressions. Look at how the eyes, nose, and mouth all change.

*Laughter* by Charles Le Brun, around 1668

## Try this!

Try using simple lines to draw faces that look:
- happy
- sad
- angry
- thoughtful

# Painting Older People

*Portrait of the Artist's Parents*
by Otto Dix, 1924

When we age our faces change. Our skin becomes wrinkled and less firm. This painting shows older people. In the painting, the artist has used lines and shadows to make the people's faces look older.

# What will you look like when you are older?

## You will need:

- *a close-up photograph of your face*
- *a close-up photograph of an older relative's face*
- *tracing paper*
- *a soft pencil*

## Instructions:

1. Find two similar-sized close-up photographs of your face and the face of an older relative. If you cannot find any suitable photographs, you could ask someone to use a camera to take photographs for you.

2. Place tracing paper over the photograph of your older family member. Now trace the lines on their face using a soft pencil.

3. Lay the tracing on top of the photograph of yourself. You should now be able to see what you might look like when you get older!

# Royal Family Portraits

Famous people, like kings and queens, paid artists to make them look wealthy and powerful. Here, **Tudor** kings Henry VII and his son Henry VIII are shown in their fine clothes. Henry VIII is **posing** in the **foreground,** making him look even more important. He also looks very heavy. Being heavy in the 1500s meant that you were wealthy, because you could afford to eat plenty of good food.

*Henry VII and Henry VIII* by Hans Holbein the Younger, around 1536–1537

**An ancient portrait**
This **portrait** was found in a **tomb** in Egypt. It was made thousands of years ago, in about 1340 B.C.E. The picture shows the ancient Egyptian king, Tutankhamen, sitting with his wife.

26

Today kings and queens are not as powerful. This portrait of the British royal family shows them relaxing together, more like a normal family. They are in a very fancy room at Buckingham Palace.

*The Royal Family: A Centenary Portrait* by John Wonnacott, 2000

**Did you notice?**

Did you notice how Prince Charles (right) and Prince William (left), the heirs to the throne, are in the foreground? This makes them seem more important.

# The Wedding Album

*The Peasant Wedding* by Pieter Brueghel the Elder, 1568

Weddings are special occasions when family and friends get together. Pieter Brueghel's painting shows a wedding feast where everyone is having fun. He packed many people into the **composition.** The whole painting is full of people doing different things.

*Bride and Groom*
by Amadeo
Modigliani,
1915–1916

This **portrait** of a bride and groom could have been painted to remind them of their big day. Even though it looks like a traditional **formal** painting, the artist has painted the bride and groom in his own style. Look how Modigliani has made the faces very long.

# Glossary

**abstract**   art not meant to look like real life, but which shows feelings or an idea

**canvas**   cloth material that many artists use to paint on

**CD-ROM**   disk used to store computer data

**composition**   how a painting is put together

**Corinth**   city in ancient Greece

**depth**   feeling of space and distance in a picture

**digital camera**   camera that stores photos electronically instead of using film

**foreground**   part of a picture that looks the closest

**formal**   carried out in a traditional way

**montage**   picture that is put together by arranging different pieces of material together

**palette**   tool used by artists to mix paint on

**portrait**   painting or photograph of a real person

**pose**   when someone puts himself or herself in a certain position in order to be drawn

**pregnant**   when a woman has a baby growing inside her

**primary color**   one of the three colors that cannot be mixed from other colors: red, blue, and yellow

**proportion**   object's size compared to another object

**solar system**   group of planets that circle the sun

**still**   photograph taken from a film

**three-dimensional**   when an object has height, width, and depth

**tomb**   place where dead people are buried

**Tudor**   name of an English royal family that ruled from 1485 to 1603

**Victorian**   from the reign of British Queen Victoria, 1837–1901

**weld**   join pieces of metal by melting them together

# More Books to Read

Heinemann Library's **How Artists Use** series:

- *Color*
- *Line and Tone*
- *Pattern and Texture*
- *Perspective*
- *Shape*

Heinemann Library's **The Life and Work of** series:

- *Alexander Calder*
- *Auguste Rodin*
- *Buonarroti Michelangelo*
- *Claude Monet*
- *Diego Rivera*
- *Edgar Degas*
- *Frederick Remington*
- *Georges Seurat*
- *Grandma Moses*
- *Henri Matisse*
- *Henry Moore*
- *Joseph Turner*
- *Leonardo da Vinci*
- *Mary Cassatt*
- *Paul Cezanne*
- *Paul Gauguin*
- *Paul Klee*
- *Pieter Brueghel*
- *Rembrandt van Rijn*
- *Vincent van Gogh*
- *Wassily Kandinsky*

# Index